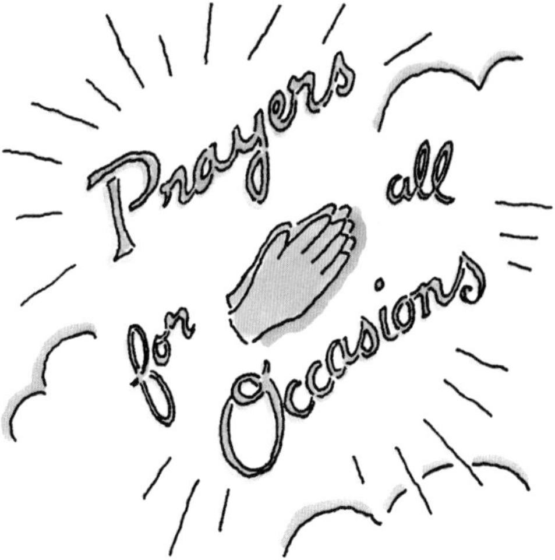
Prayers
for
all
Occasions

Prayers for all Occasions

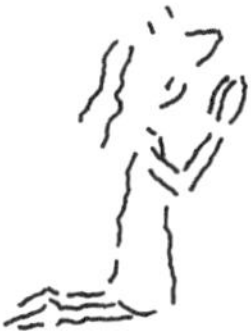

Sanctuary
and
Salvation
at your
Fingertips!

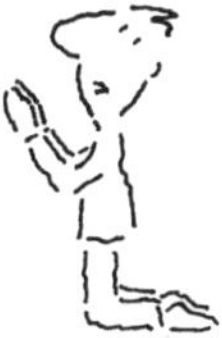

by Monica Sheehan

RUNNING PRESS
PHILADELPHIA · LONDON

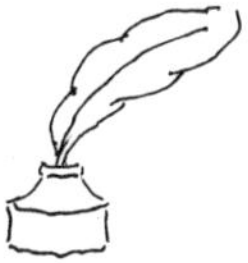

Dedication

To the Holy Quinity

Mary Jane Kroon
Sarah Kroon Chiles
Nora Sheehan
Joan Curley
Susie McCabe

... and all the others that had faith in this
Patron Saint of Missed Deadlines.

9   8   7   6   5   4   3   2   1
Digit on the right indicates the number of this printing

Library of Congress Control Number: 2007920543

ISBN 13: 978-0-7624-3135-9
ISBN 10: 0-7624-3135-0

Conceived, written, and illustrated by Monica Sheehan
Produced exclusively for Running Press Book Publishers by:
Herter Studio
432 Elizabeth Street
San Francisco, CA

This book may be ordered by mail from the publisher.
Please include $2.50 for postage and handling.
But try your bookstore first!

Running Press Book Publishers
2300 Chestnut Street
Philadelphia, Pennsylvania 19103-4371

Visit us on the web!
www.runningpress.com

Acknowledgements

Special thanks to these generous—
but more importantly—funny people,
who helped me write this book...

Michael Kroon
Chris Curley
Michael & Margaret Sheehan
Andrew Sheehan
John & Chris Murray
Megan Buckalew
Jon Kleiman
Kevin Byrne
Linda Mann
Al Ellenberg
and Georgio!

(It took a village... literally.)

Contents

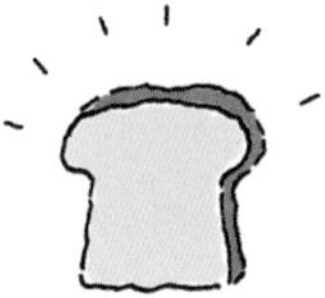

Daily Bread

Prayers for Everyday Life

Exhaustion Prayer

———◄•►———

God, grant me the
power
To get out of this
shower.

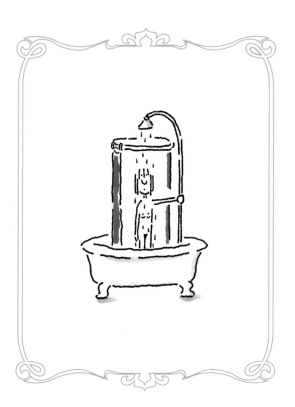

Let There Be Milk

———◄•►———

Without milk for my coffee,
I will die.
On your power, I will rely.

(Remember what you did with
the loaves and the fishes.)

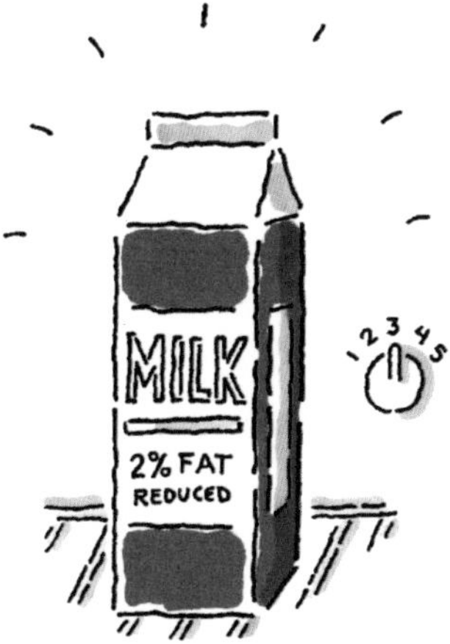
MILK
2% FAT
REDUCED
1 2 3 4 5

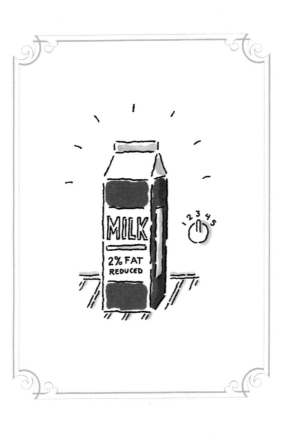

Late *for* Work
Prayer

—◄•►—

O God, please let this train

be an Express,

And make this wrinkled suit

look pressed.

So I can prove to my boss—

I'm not a mess.

Prayer *for* Lost Keys

—◆—

Restore my memory
so my keys I can find,
Before I lose my
freakin' mind.

Prayer *for*
a Parking Spot

———◄•►———

O dear Lord, it's in You

that I believe.

Prove that you love me,

and make someone leave.

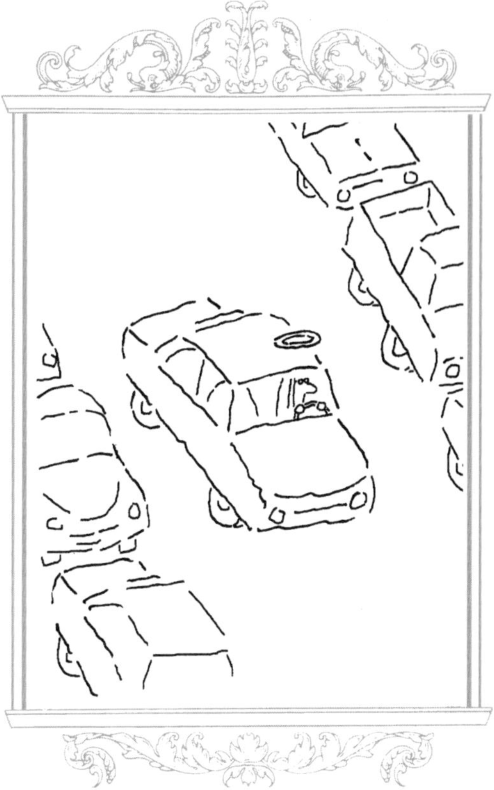

Multiple Choice
White Lie Forgiveness Prayer

Lord, forgive me for lying about

_____
(Insert your white lie here)

A. Being busy.
B. Not feeling well.
C. Paying the bill.
D. Wanting to get together.
E. Not being home.
F. Returning the video.
G. Not having my cellphone on.
H. Other

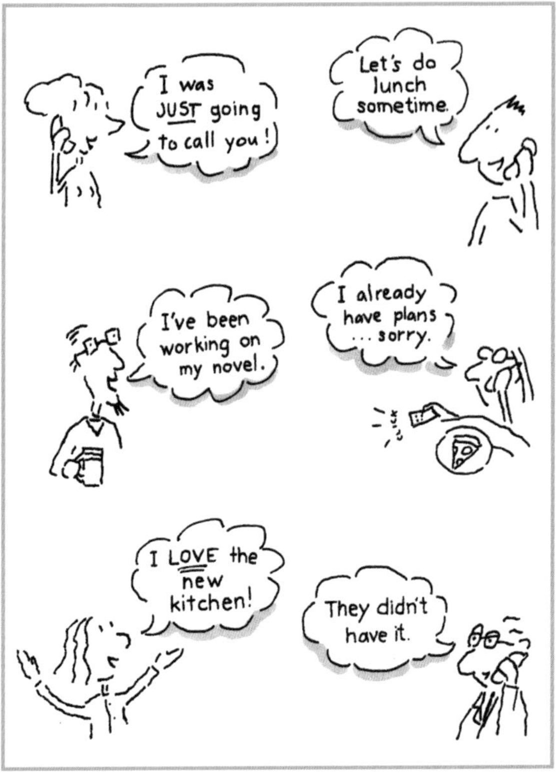
I was JUST going to call you!
Let's do lunch sometime.
I've been working on my novel.
I already have plans ... sorry.
I LOVE the new kitchen!
They didn't have it.

O Lord, Hear Our Horn

---◆►---

Have mercy, O Lord, and hear our horn.
Stuck in this traffic has got us worn.
And now we have used
Your name in vain,
Because some guy cut into our lane.

Forgive us please, God, for our sin.
(But he's the jerk for cutting in.)

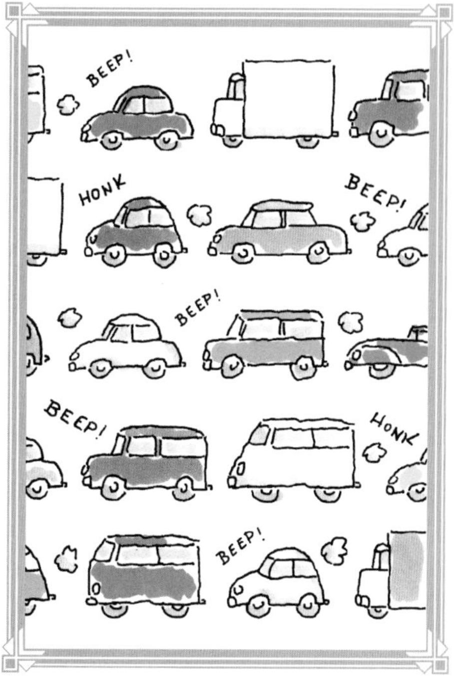
BEEP!
HONK
BEEP!
BEEP!
BEEP!
HONK
BEEP!

Check Out Line
Serenity Prayer

———◄•►———

God, grant me the serenity
to stand on this check out line,
the courage to face price checks
and the wisdom to know when
to change lanes.

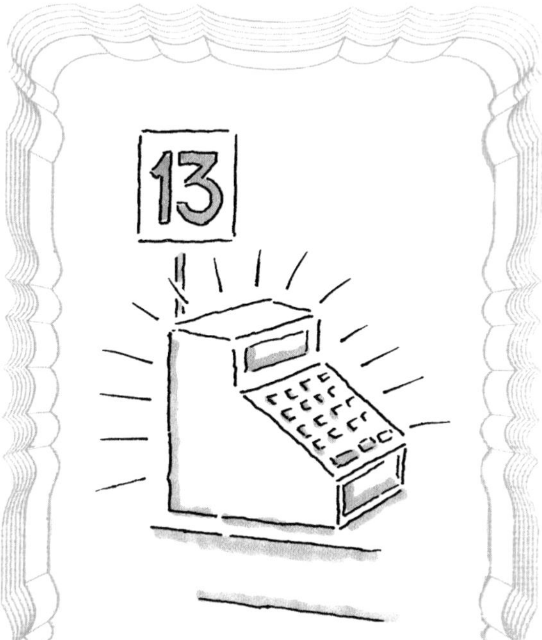
13

Annoying Neighbor
Prayer

———◄•►———

By day they're rude.

By night they're noisy.

Please, God,

banish them to Boise.

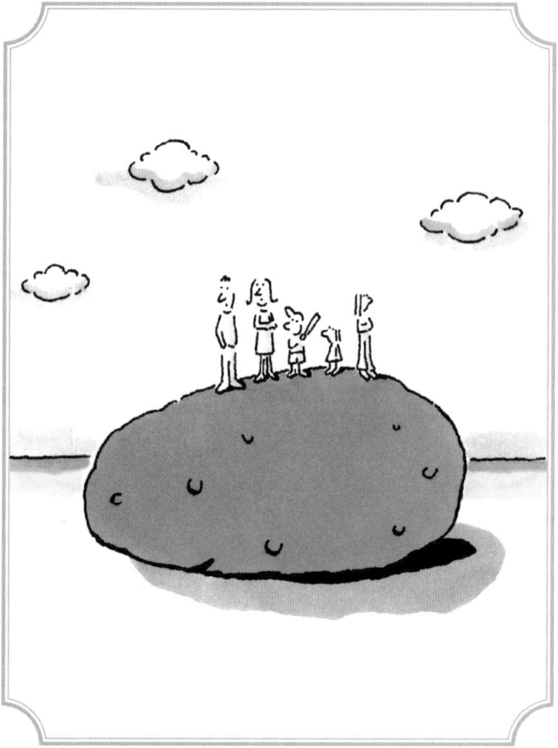

The Flossing Prayer

—◄•►—

O dear God, please save me
My will to floss evades me.
Through your holy intercession
Protect me from gum recession.

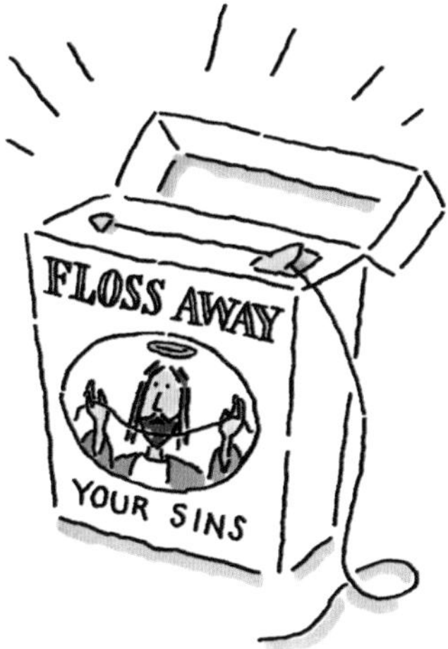
FLOSS AWAY
YOUR SINS

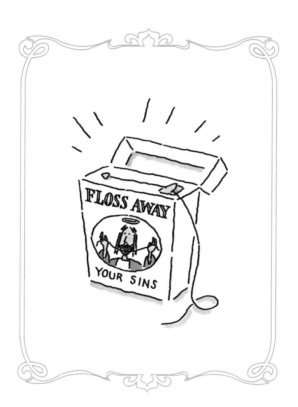

Prayer *for* Eight Hours

—◄•►—

O Lord, put me in a
heavenly coma,
And don't let this mind
of mine roma.

I ask this through Christ our Lord,
Ambien

RIP
me
IT'S TIED!

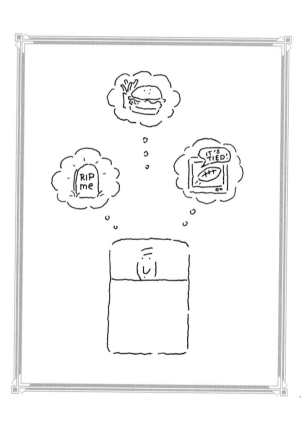

Hail Mary Passes

———◄•►———

Prayers for a Little Divine Intervention

Prayer to
The Refrigerator

O Lord, take-out I can't taketh no more,
Let there be food when I open this door.
To the store I can't go
I'm way too tired.
Just let there be something
that's not expired.

Prayer *to* Obtain Favors

———◄•►———

Dear Lord,

These shoes I cannot afford.

But without them, I shall

be bored.

Prayer for a Bathroom

——◄•►——

Hurry God, my bladder is busting—
Find me a bathroom
that's not too disgusting.

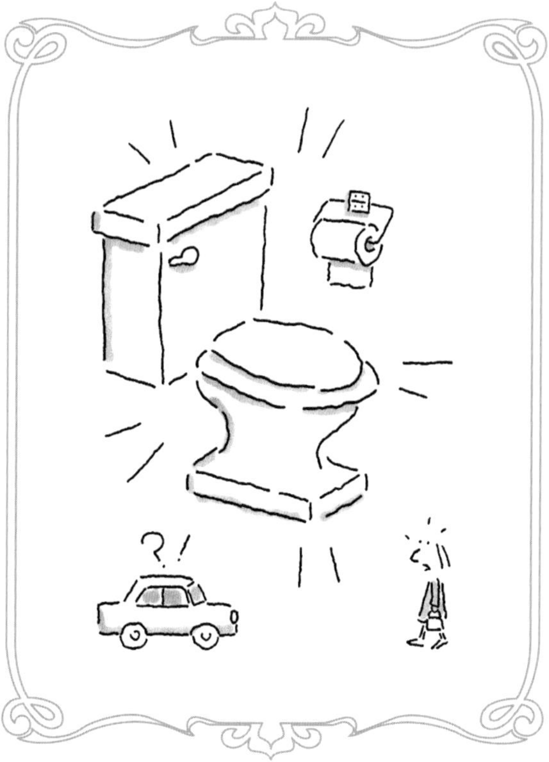

Prayer for the Lost

Which way should we go?
Help us choose it.
O God Almighty,
Before we lose it.

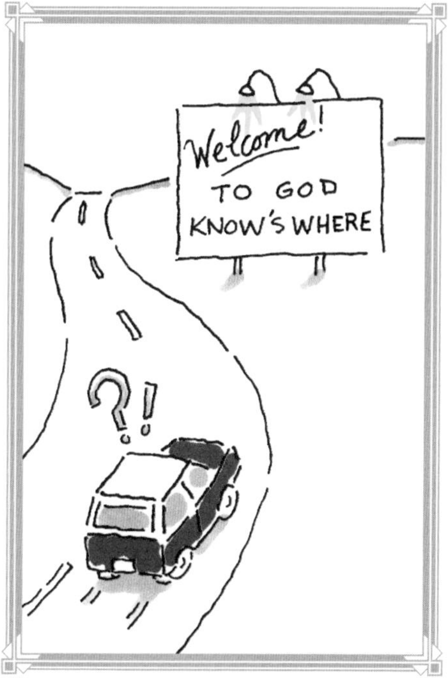
Welcome!
TO GOD
KNOW'S WHERE

The "Let It Be Canceled" Prayer

———•———

This _event name_ has felt

like a curse all week.

O Holy One, your power I seek.

Please let my joy

eternally spring—

Grant me "the call"

that cancels this thing.

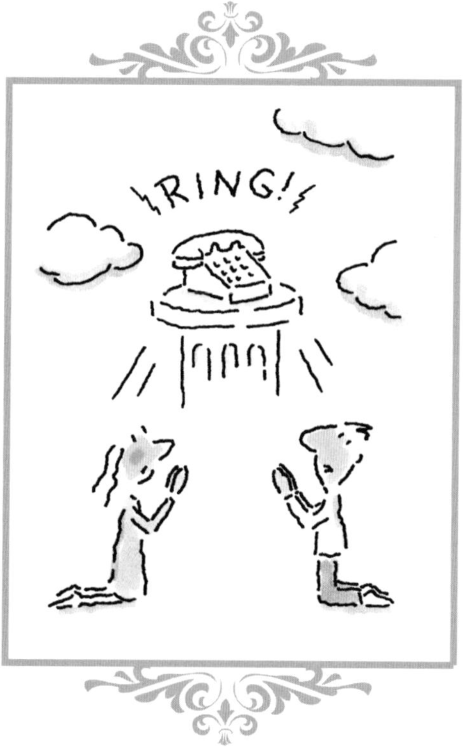
RING!

To Our Lady *of* Perpetual Disappointment

———◄•►———

Thanks for letting my rent check bounce.

Thanks for the parking ticket.

Thanks for the lame family.

Thanks for letting it rain on my one day off.

Thanks for another pathetic relationship.

Thanks for the cold sore.

Gimme a break, God.

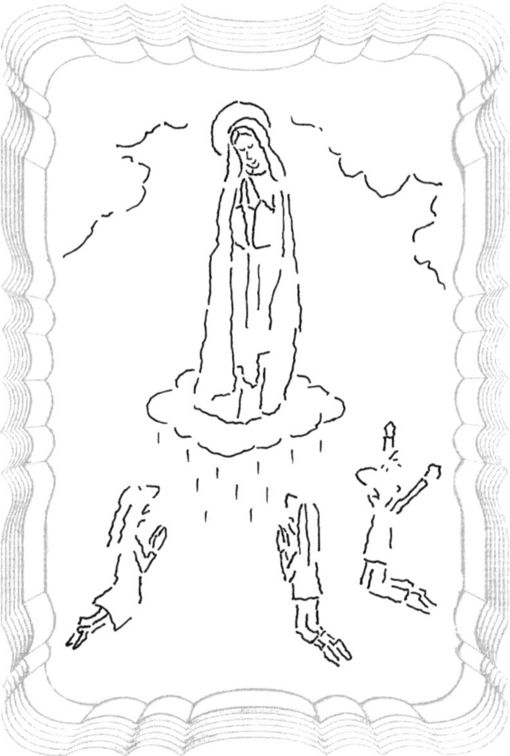

The
"What's Their Name"
Prayer

———◄•►———

God help me, this is truly insane,

I cannot remember this guy's name.

O dear Lord, please give me

a hunch—

Before he wants to meet for lunch.

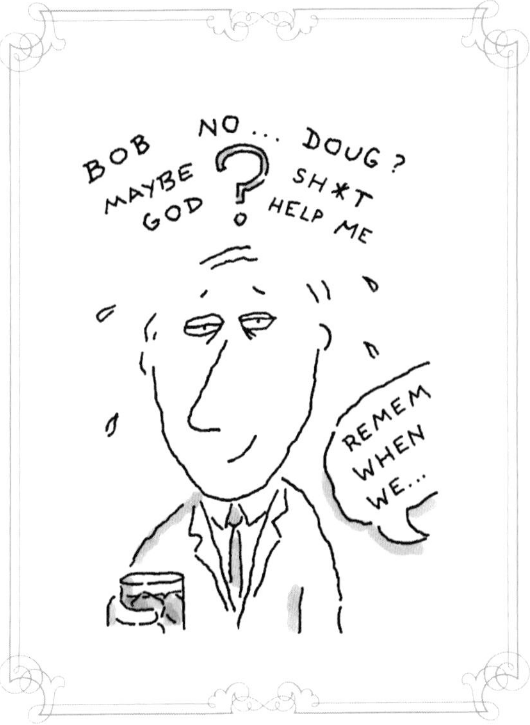
BOB NO... DOUG?
MAYBE GOD
SH*T HELP ME
REMEM WHEN WE...

Out *of* Shape Prayer

———◄•►———

Bless me Father for I
have sinned.
It has been two months since
I've gone to the gym.

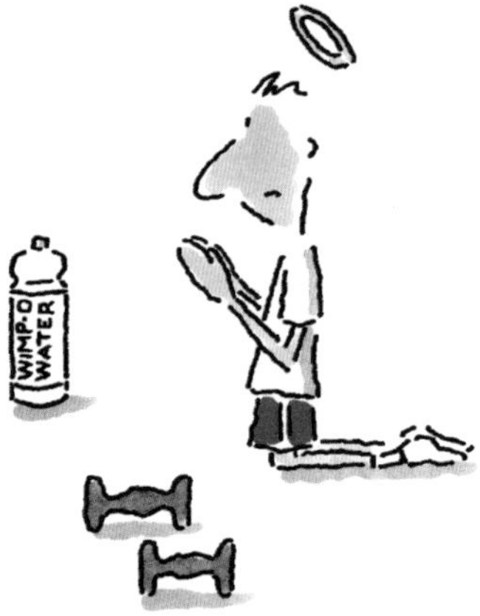
WIMP-O
WATER

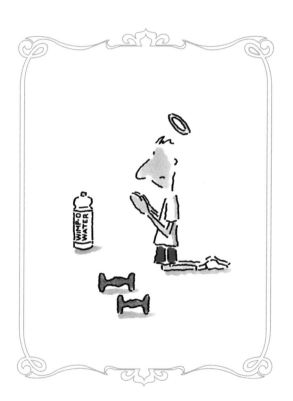

Prayer for
the Doubting Hostess

——◄•►——

Lord, make me an instrument of entertaining.

Where there is cheese, let me bring crackers;

Where there is crudite, dip;

Where there is a coat, a hanger;

Where there is a margarita, salt;

And where there is coffee, milk.

O Divine Master,

send this hostess to heaven,

And grant that they're out

of this house by eleven.

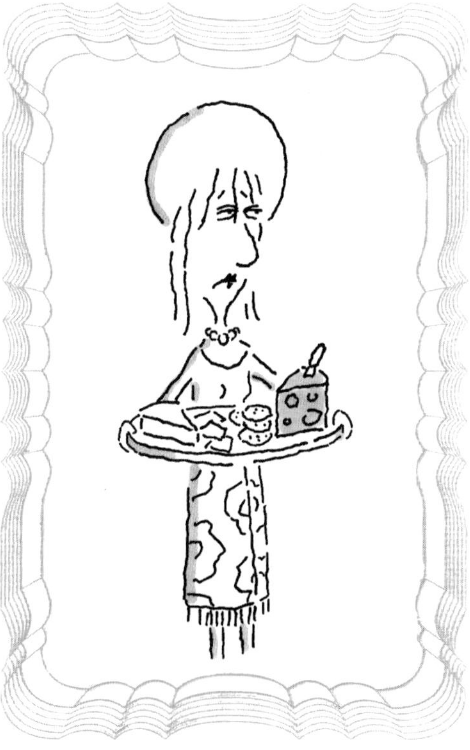

Viewing Protection
Prayer

———◄•►———

Keep sacred my popcorn and

my perfect view,

Deliver me from talkers

and big hair-dos.

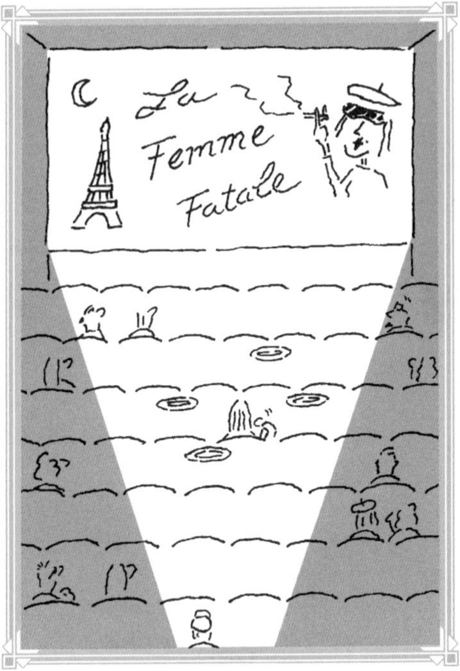
La
Femme
Fatale

Cable Outage Prayer

———◄•►———

Dear God, if you are willing
and able,
Have mercy on us, and
"Let there be cable."

The Lottery Prayer

Oh Lord, won't you let me win the lottery?
My friends all have money,
how 'bout some for me.
Want a house on the hill, with a hi-def TV,
So Lord, won't you let me win the lottery?

Prayer *for* Car Trouble

———◄·►———

Please God, let that noise
just be my muffler—
And not my car ready to blow up.

Grant me safe haven
in my driveway,
And at church on Sunday, I'll show up.

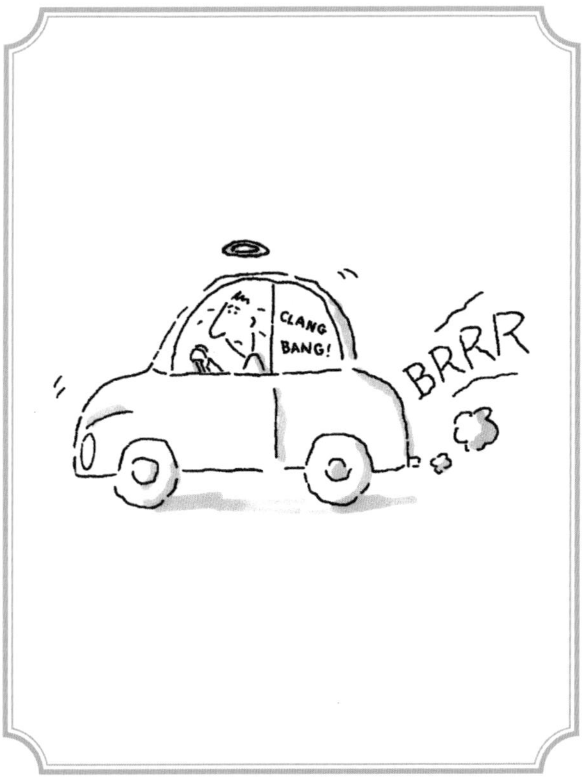
CLANG
BANG!
BRRR

The
"I Can't Make It" Call
Prayer

———•>———

O dear Lord,
I know this sounds mean,
But please let me get
the answering machine.

Parking Lot
Amnesia Prayer

———◄•►———

Angel sent by God to guide me,
Be my light and walk beside me.
Help me kindly to recall
Where I parked at this stupid Mall.

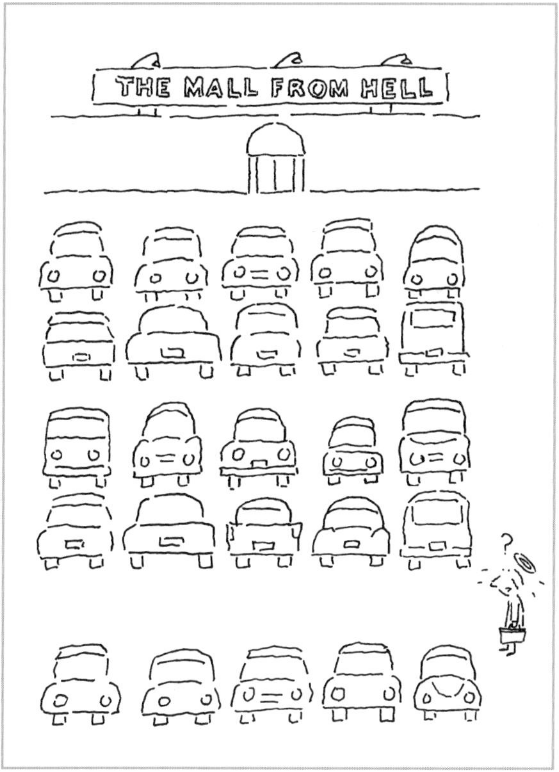
THE MALL FROM HELL
?

The Depressing Room
Prayer

—◄•►—

Jesus Christ, my one
true savior,
May I ask you a small favor?

Please let these fit.

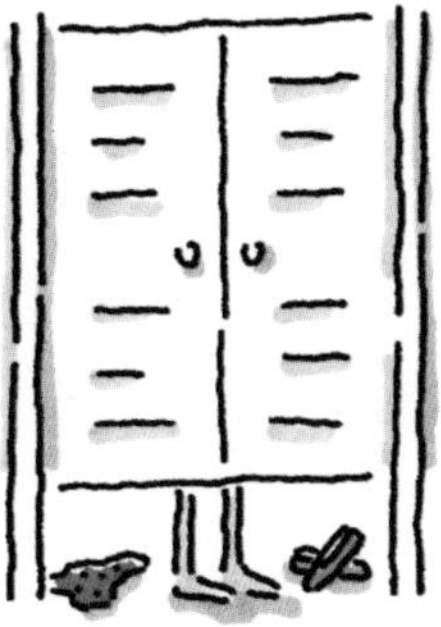

Luck Be Our Lady

———◄•►———

Hail Mary, full of grace,
You gave me a king,
Now deal me an ace.

*Pray for us gamblers now
and in the hour of our bets.
Amen*

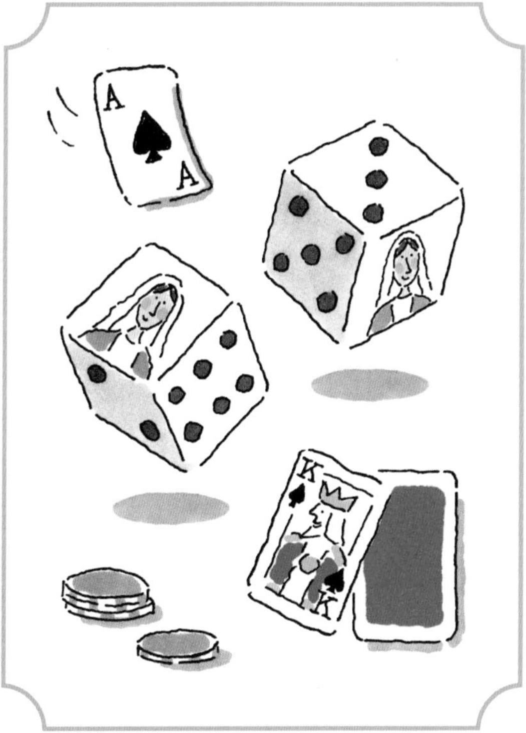

Prayer for
The Computer Illiterate

———◄•►———

I know my salvation will come
in the end.
Till then let this computer
be my friend.

Snow Day Prayers

—◄•►—

Ages: 5 and up

The forecast says snow,
please let it be true.
This time God—
You gotta come through.
Because my homework,
I didn't do.

Ages: 21 and up

To not go to work, for this, I pray.
Please God, send a blizzard my way.
(I need an un-national holiday.)

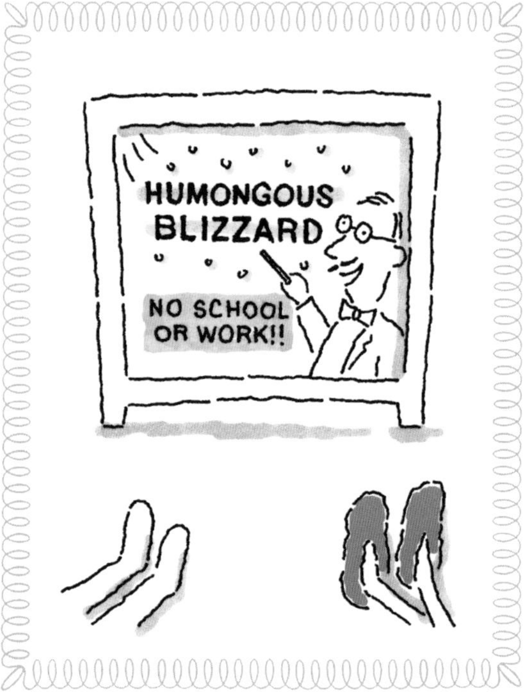
HUMONGOUS BLIZZARD
NO SCHOOL OR WORK!!

Abstinence Alley

—◄•►—

Lead Us Not into Temptation…

Hangover Helper

———◄•►———

God, if you help me through this day,
I promise,
I will change my ways, and live like
the Amish.

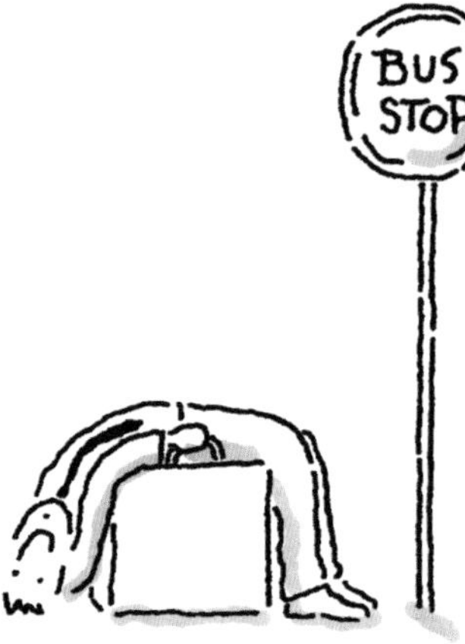
BUS
STOP

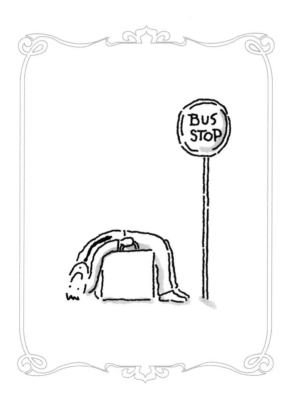

The Entenmann's Abstinence Prayer

---◆►---

At the counter, just one
more sliver,
O Lord, from this crumb cake
please deliver.

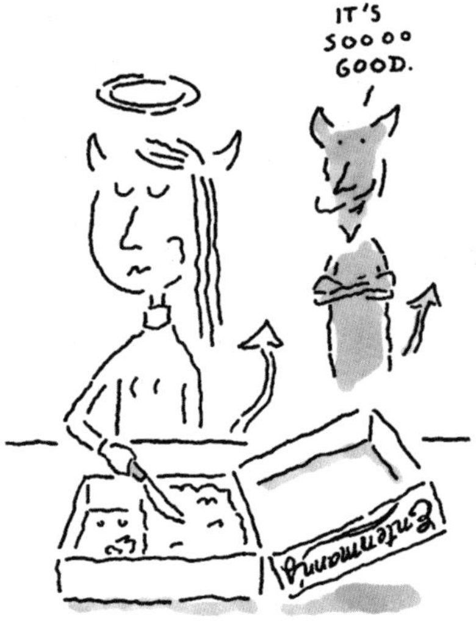
IT'S SOOOO GOOD.
Entenmann's

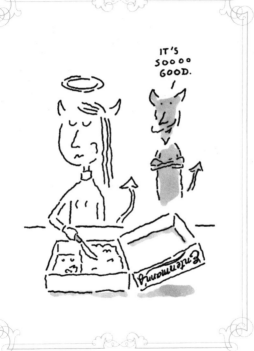

Candy Confession

———◄•►———

Dear Lord, I come to you
with darkness in my soul,
I just ate my
seventeenth Tootsie Roll.

The Single Serving Prayer

Dear Lord, this ice cream I must
learn to ration.
Please help me eat it in a
normal fashion.
Grant me the wisdom of portion control,
To let me actually use a bowl.

And lead me not into temptation,
Back to the land of refrigeration.
Let me choose instead—
my figure's preservation.

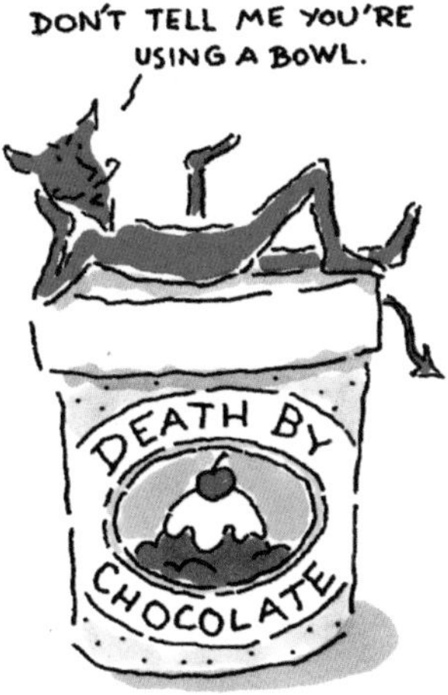
DON'T TELL ME YOU'RE USING A BOWL.
DEATH BY CHOCOLATE

Prayer Not to Eat
The Bread

———◄•►———

O Lord, I beseech
Don't let these hands,
To that basket reach.

Amen.

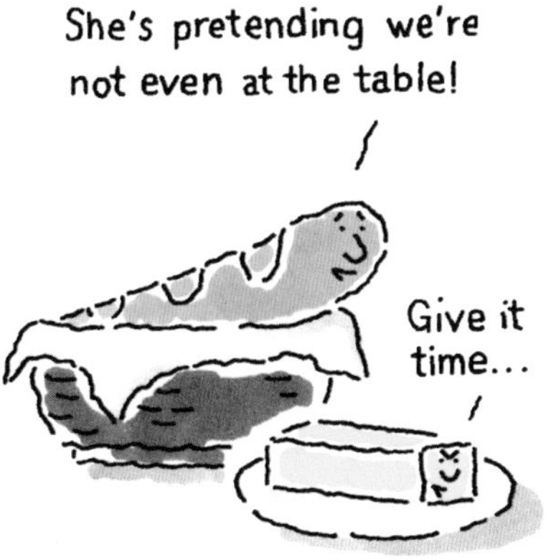
She's pretending we're not even at the table!
Give it time...

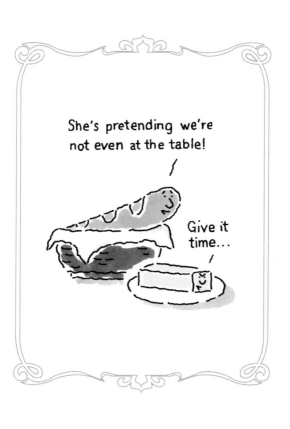

The Scale Prayer

———◄•►———

Pray for us
sinners,
Who ate big
dinners.

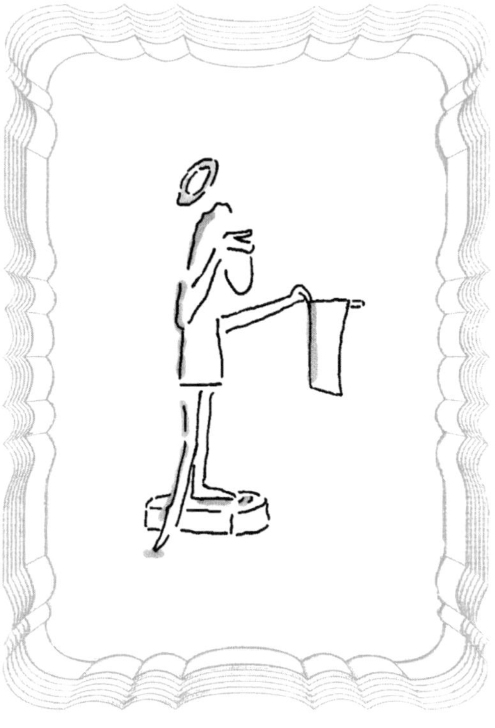

The Smoker's Creed

———◄•►———

Dear God, let me make it
through some way,
Without lighting up again today.
Lord keep away this habit's nag,
But let me have—
just one more drag...
(and one more drag after that.)

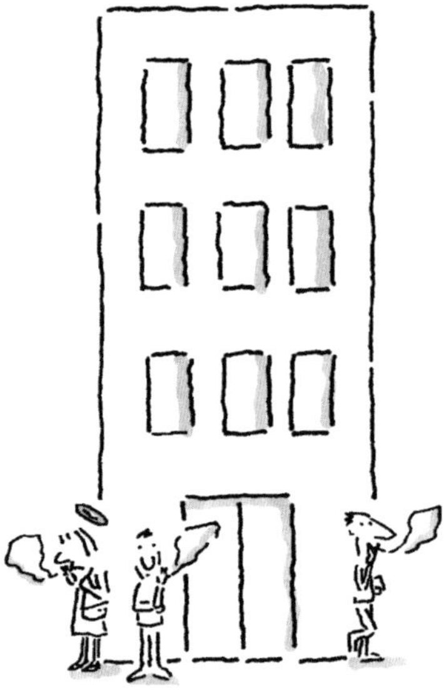

Prayers for Singles

— ◀ ◆ ▶ —

Salvation for One, Please

The Underwear Prayer

—◄•►—

Dear Lord, it's an easy
one today,
Clean underwear is for
what I pray.

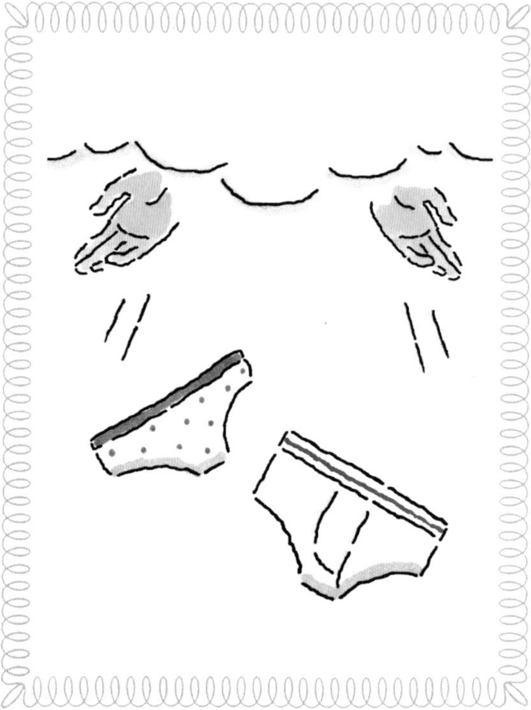

Prayer for Protection from Ex-boyfriends

———◄•►———

Angel of Mercy, my guardian

from fear,

That jerk I dated is in this

restaurant here.

Please don't let him see me.

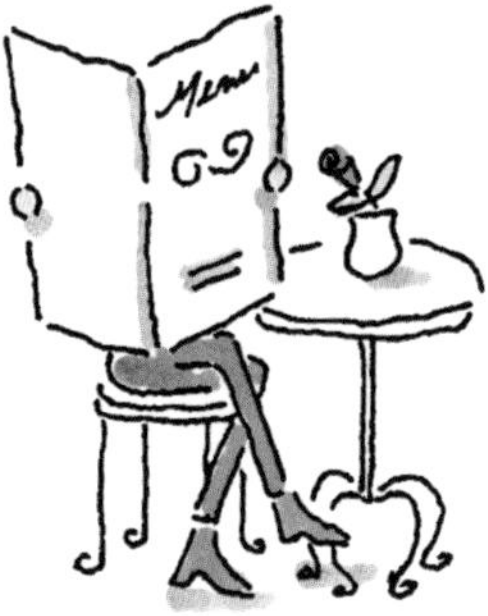
Menu

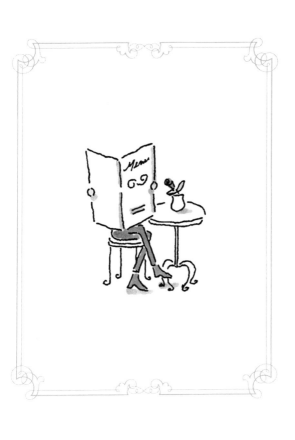

Protection from
Ex-girlfriends

——◄·►——

All powerful God,
let me disappear.
That nutcase I dated is
at the bar here.

Please don't let her want to talk.

Please, Let Him Call
Responsorial Psalm

———◄•►———

Make me stop staring into space
And let me join the human race.
refrain:
Please, let him call.

We have a good thing
Let that phone ring.
refrain:
Please let him call.

God, release this paralysis—
and keep me from analysis.
refrain:
Please let him call.

Please, Let Him Call
(continued)

What's the big deal?
Is this guy for real?
refrain:
Please let him call.

Don't let me be another notch,
Excuse me while I get a scotch.
refrain:
Please let him call.

OK God, I'll ask one more time—
I'll count to ten, then let it chyme.
refrain:
Please let him call.

Internet Dating Prayer

———◄•►———

Grant me the strength to endure
yet another internet date.
And don't let this photograph
be from 1988.

Prayer for
Love or Money

——◄·►——

God, if you should grant me
Love or Money,
At this point, either one is fine.

(and both, of course, would be divine)

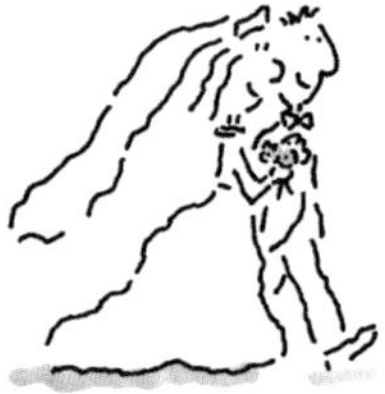

Love "or" Money

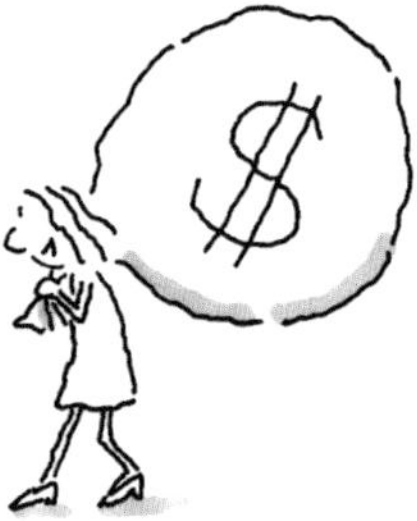
$

Prayers for Families

——◆——

Heaven Help Us

Mother Visitation Prayer

———◄•►———

From my past, she's sure to
drop a bomb,
Please help me to
"Let go, let Mom."

Grace

—◂•▸—

Give us this day
our multi-grain bread,
Soup without salt,
and carbs without dread.

Give us soy at each meal,
with no trans fat food,
And God, somehow please,
let us think it tastes good.

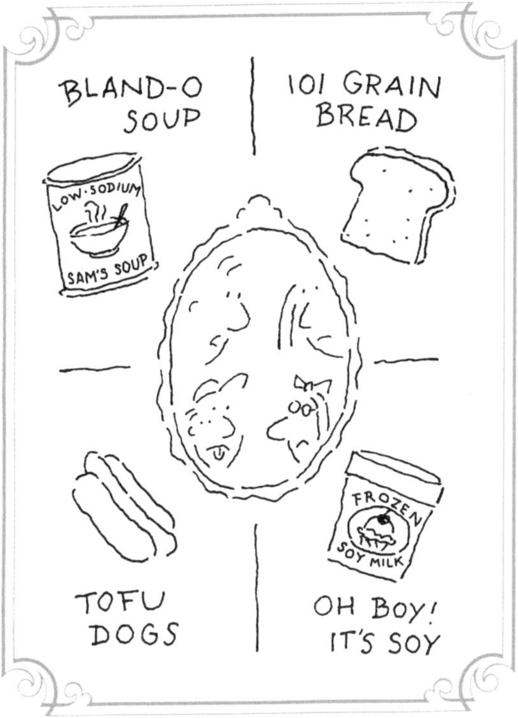

BLAND-O SOUP
LOW-SODIUM
SAM'S SOUP
101 GRAIN BREAD
FROZEN
SOY MILK
TOFU DOGS
OH BOY! IT'S SOY

Prayer to Obtain a Babysitter

———◄•►———

Help me God,

To find the babysitter I needeth.

Margaritas tonight,

I want to drinketh.

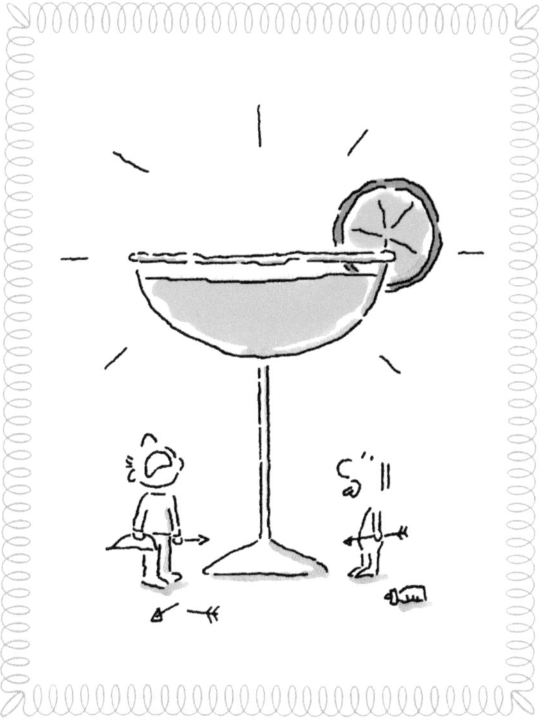

Lord, Hear Our Prayer

A Few of Many Parents' Prayers

———◄•►———

Johnny needs a new pair of $100.00 shoes,
Deliver us please,
from these cash machine blues.
refrain:
Lord, hear our prayer.

Four semesters of being cool,
We pray dear God, no summer school.
refrain:
Lord, hear our prayer.

I pray the tattoo on my daughter's back
Won't give my wife and I a heart attack.
refrain:
Lord, hear our prayer.

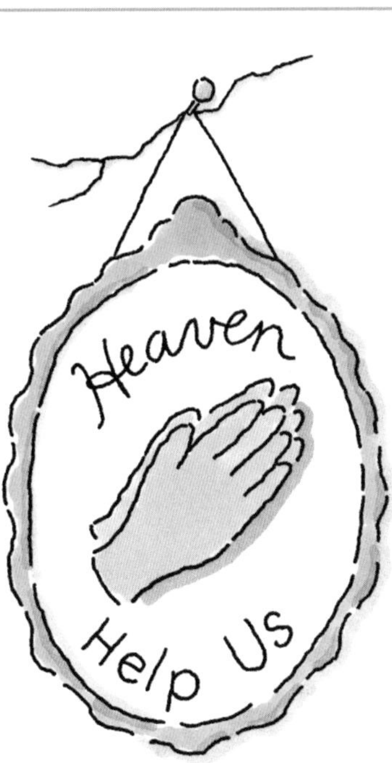
Heaven
Help Us

Prayer for New Parents

———◄•►———

O Heavenly Father
put this baby to bed,
So we don't look like
the walking dead.

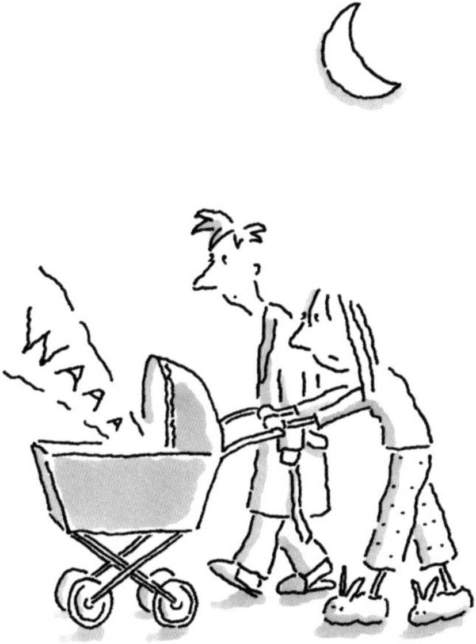
WAAA

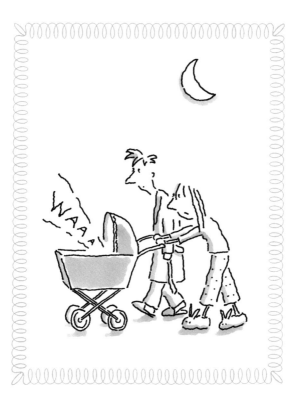

Anti-Aging Prayers

—◄•►—

For Those Who Could Use a Lift

The Botox Creed

Keep our lines and crowsfeet
at bay,
O Mary we implore—
Don't let our Botox go away,
Until we can afford some more.

Prayer for Hair

——◄•►——

Dear God, I know we must

all carry a cross.

Please— don't let mine be

male-pattern hair loss.

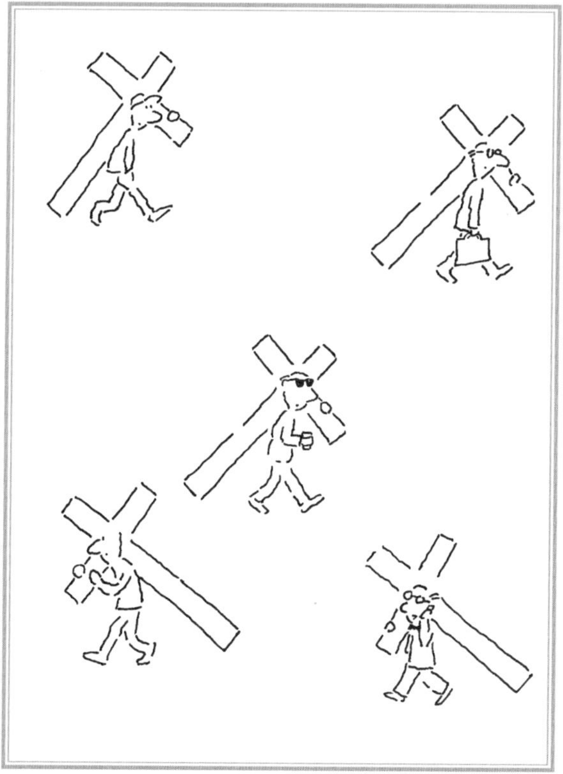

The Descent of
the Derriere Prayer

—◀•▶—

Lord, if you could be so kind

With hands that helped

heal the blind,

To lift up this sagging behind.

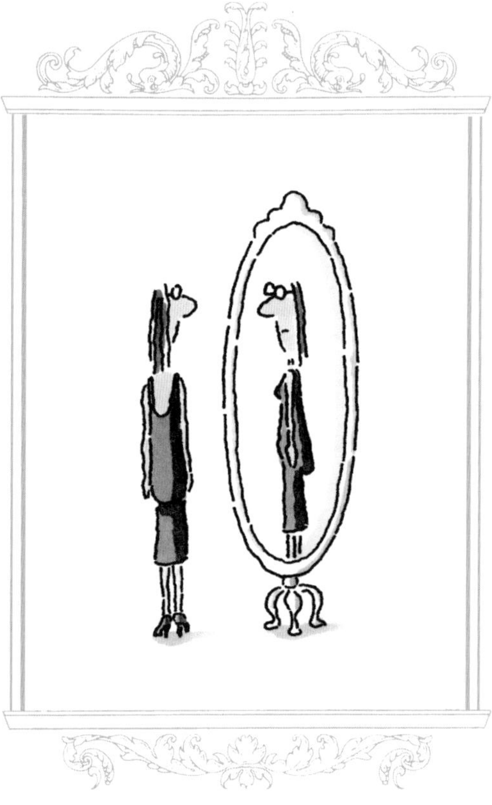

Memory Prayer

—◄•►—

Please make a deposit in my
memory bank,
So when I'm dying I know
who to thank.

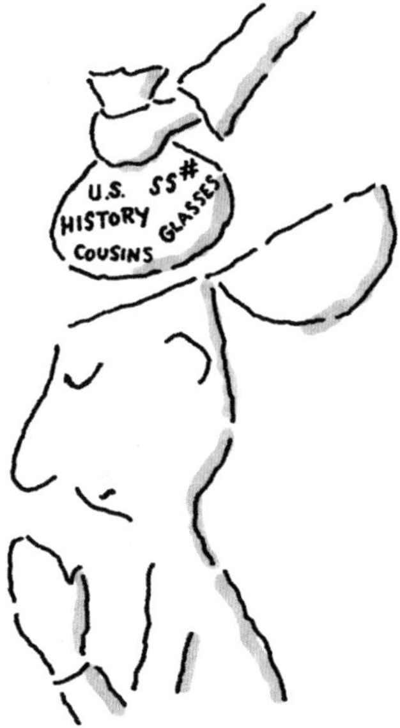
U.S.
SS#
HISTORY
GLASSES
COUSINS

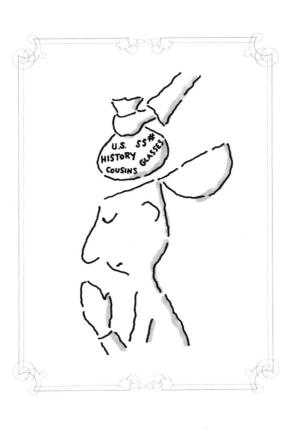

The End

Thank God.